INCOME MULTIPLICITY AND LIBERATION FROM FOREIGN CURRENCY CONTROLS

"STRATEGIES FOR ECONOMIC AUTONOMY IN A WORLD OF CURRENCY RESTRAINTS"

BLESS P. WALTON

TABLE OF CONTENTS

CHAPTER 1

INTRODUCTION

1.1 Background

In the ever-evolving landscape of global economics, the concept of economic autonomy has emerged as a critical factor in the pursuit of national prosperity and resilience. Nations across the world navigate complex economic terrains influenced by international markets, trade dependencies, and, significantly, foreign currency controls.

Understanding the nuances of these controls and formulating strategies for economic autonomy are pivotal for nations striving to assert their financial independence.

The background of this book lies in the recognition of the profound impact that foreign currency controls can exert on a nation's economic stability and growth. Over the years, numerous countries have faced the challenges posed by stringent currency restrictions, which have led to economic vulnerabilities and hindered development. This chapter sets the stage by delving into the historical context and contemporary relevance of the issues surrounding foreign currency controls.

In tracing the historical roots, we uncover instances where nations grappled with the consequences of currency controls and the subsequent implications on their economic trajectories. The examination of past experiences serves as a valuable guide, offering insights into both successful strategies and pitfalls to avoid in the pursuit of economic autonomy.

1.2 Rationale for Economic Autonomy

The rationale for economic autonomy stems from the imperative to safeguard a nation's economic interests in an interconnected global economy. Economic interdependence can be a double-edged sword, as it opens up avenues for growth and collaboration but also exposes nations to external shocks and vulnerabilities.

As such, the pursuit of economic autonomy becomes not merely a nationalistic endeavor but a pragmatic strategy to ensure resilience in the face of global economic uncertainties.

This section explores the multifaceted reasons for prioritizing economic autonomy. Beyond the desire for political sovereignty, economic autonomy provides nations with the flexibility to design and implement policies that cater to their specific needs and aspirations. Moreover, it serves as a buffer against external economic pressures, enabling countries to weather storms such as currency fluctuations, trade imbalances, and financial crises.

The rationale for economic autonomy is deeply intertwined with the concept of self-determination. Nations aspire not only to control their economic destinies but also to create environments conducive to sustainable development, job creation, and improved standards of living for their citizens. By understanding the underlying motivations for pursuing economic autonomy, we can better appreciate the urgency and importance of the strategies presented in subsequent chapters.

1.3 Overview of Foreign Currency Controls

Foreign currency controls represent a significant aspect of international economic relations, encompassing a range of policies and measures implemented by nations to regulate the flow of currency across borders. These controls can take various forms, including capital controls, exchange rate restrictions, and limits on foreign transactions. Understanding the mechanics and implications of these controls is crucial for policymakers, economists, and business leaders alike.

This section provides a comprehensive overview of foreign currency controls, examining the historical evolution of such measures and their impact on different economies. We explore the reasons behind the imposition of currency controls, whether to stabilize exchange rates, prevent capital flight, or address trade imbalances. The chapter also considers the challenges associated with these controls, including potential distortions in domestic markets, reduced foreign investment, and constraints on economic growth.

By unraveling the complexities of foreign currency controls, we aim to equip readers with a nuanced understanding of the dynamics at play. This knowledge serves as the foundation for the subsequent chapters, where strategies for navigating and liberating from these controls will be explored in detail.

1.4 Objectives of the Book

As we embark on this exploration of income multiplicity and liberation from foreign currency controls, the objectives of this book come into focus. The primary goal is to provide a comprehensive and actionable guide for nations seeking to enhance their economic autonomy in the face of currency restraints. The specific objectives include:

- Knowledge Enhancement: To deepen the reader's understanding of the historical context, current challenges, and future implications of foreign currency controls on national economies.

- Strategic Insights: To offer strategic insights into the concept of income multiplicity as a means to diversify and strengthen a nation's economic base, thereby mitigating the impact of currency controls.

- Case Studies: To analyze and draw lessons from the experiences of nations that have successfully achieved economic autonomy, examining their policies, challenges faced, and the outcomes of their strategies.

- Policy Recommendations: To provide practical policy recommendations for governments and policymakers, focusing on legal and regulatory considerations, the development of domestic financial systems, entrepreneurship promotion, and trade alliances.

- Global Perspective: To encourage a global perspective on economic autonomy, recognizing the interconnectedness of nations and the potential for collaborative efforts to overcome common challenges.

In pursuing these objectives, this book aims to serve as a valuable resource for academics, policymakers, business leaders, and anyone interested in the intricate interplay between economic autonomy and foreign currency controls. By addressing these issues comprehensively, we aspire to contribute to the discourse on sustainable economic development in a world marked by currency restraints and global uncertainties.

CHAPTER 2

UNDERSTANDING FOREIGN CURRENCY CONTROLS

2.1 Definition and Types of Currency Controls

Foreign currency controls, often employed by nations as a tool to manage their economies, represent a set of policies and regulations designed to govern the flow of currency across national borders. These controls can manifest in various forms, each serving a specific purpose in the economic landscape.

Understanding the nuances of currency controls is essential for comprehending their impact on economic stability and for formulating effective strategies for economic autonomy.

2.1.1 Definition

At its core, currency controls encompass a range of measures imposed by governments to monitor, restrict, or regulate the movement of capital and currency within and beyond their borders. These measures can include restrictions on foreign exchange transactions, limits on the amount of currency that individuals and businesses can hold, and regulations governing international capital flows.

2.1.2 Types of Currency Controls

Currency controls can take several forms, each addressing specific economic concerns:

a. Capital Controls: These measures restrict the flow of capital across borders, often aiming to prevent speculative attacks on a nation's currency. Capital controls may involve limitations on the repatriation of profits, restrictions on foreign investment, or the imposition of transaction taxes.

b. Exchange Rate Controls: Governments may intervene in the foreign exchange market to stabilize or manipulate their currency's value. This can involve fixed or pegged exchange rate systems, where the value of the domestic currency is tied to another currency or a basket of currencies.

c. Transaction Controls: Imposing restrictions on certain types of international transactions is another common form of currency control. This may include limitations on imports and exports, restrictions on the use of foreign currency for domestic transactions, or requirements for approval before engaging in specific international trade activities.

Understanding the distinctions among these types of controls is crucial for dissecting their impact on economic systems and formulating tailored strategies for economic autonomy.

2.2 Historical Context of Currency Restraints

To appreciate the significance of foreign currency controls, it is imperative to examine their historical context. Throughout history, nations have grappled with economic challenges that prompted the implementation of currency controls. From the gold standard era to the post-World War II Bretton Woods system, the evolution of currency controls reflects the shifting dynamics of global economics.

2.2.1 The Gold Standard and Pre-World War II Era

The gold standard, prevalent in the 19th and early 20th centuries, pegged the value of national currencies to a specific quantity of gold. While providing stability, it constrained the ability of governments to address economic downturns through monetary policy. The Great Depression of the 1930s saw countries resorting to protectionist measures and currency controls to shield their economies.

2.2.2 Bretton Woods System and Its Unraveling

The Bretton Woods system, established in 1944, aimed to stabilize post-war economies by pegging major currencies to the U.S. dollar, which, thus, was connected to gold. However, the system faced challenges, leading to the suspension of the gold convertibility of the U.S. dollar in 1971. This marked a pivotal moment, as nations shifted towards floating exchange rates and the subsequent adoption of various currency controls to manage economic uncertainties.

2.2.3 Post-Bretton Woods Era and Globalization

The breakdown of the Bretton Woods system paved the way for increased financial globalization. Nations, facing volatility in exchange rates and capital flows, began implementing diverse currency controls to safeguard their economies. The historical context underscores the adaptive nature of currency controls, evolving in response to changing economic paradigms.

2.3 Impact of Foreign Currency Controls on Economic Stability

Currency controls exert a profound influence on a nation's economic stability, shaping the macroeconomic environment and influencing key indicators. Understanding the impact of these controls is essential for crafting effective strategies to navigate and, where possible, liberate from their constraints.

2.3.1 Exchange Rate Stability vs. Flexibility

Currency controls can impact exchange rates, either by stabilizing them through interventions or by allowing for market-driven fluctuations. Stable exchange rates provide certainty for businesses and investors but may limit a nation's ability to adjust to economic shocks. Flexible exchange rates, on the other hand, can enhance competitiveness but may lead to volatility.

2.3.2 Capital Flows and Investment

Capital controls directly affect the flow of investment in and out of a country. While capital controls can shield a nation from speculative attacks and sudden outflows, they may also deter foreign investment and limit access to global capital markets. Striking the right balance is crucial to foster economic growth without exposing the economy to excessive risks.

2.3.3 Trade Balances and Economic Growth

Currency controls can influence a nation's trade balances by affecting the competitiveness of its exports and the cost of imports. A well-calibrated approach to currency controls can support a positive trade balance, contributing to economic growth. However, overly restrictive controls may lead to inefficiencies and hinder the development of international trade relations.

2.4 Case Studies of Countries with Stringent Controls

Examining case studies of countries that have implemented stringent currency controls provides valuable insights into the challenges and opportunities associated with such measures.

2.4.1 China: Managed Exchange Rates and Capital Controls

China, with its managed exchange rate system and extensive capital controls, has successfully navigated economic challenges while sustaining rapid growth. By carefully controlling its currency's value and limiting capital flows, China has maintained stability and avoided some of the pitfalls associated with volatile exchange rates.

2.4.2 Argentina: Struggles with Exchange Rate Volatility

Argentina has faced recurring economic crises, partly attributed to challenges in managing its exchange rate. While implementing various currency controls, the country has grappled with issues of inflation, capital flight, and economic instability, highlighting the complexities associated with finding the right balance.

2.4.3 Switzerland: Balancing Act in a Globalized Economy

Switzerland has implemented a unique set of currency controls to balance the influx of capital and maintain the competitiveness of its exports. The country's experience showcases the importance of adapting currency controls to the specific needs of an economy and the challenges posed by global economic interconnectedness.

These case studies underscore the diverse approaches nations take in implementing currency controls and the varying degrees of success they achieve. By examining both positive and negative outcomes, policymakers and economists can distill valuable lessons applicable to the formulation of effective economic autonomy strategies.

In conclusion, this chapter provides a comprehensive understanding of foreign currency controls by delving into their definitions, types, historical context, and impact on economic stability. The exploration of case studies offers a practical lens through which readers can grasp the real-world implications of currency controls, laying the groundwork for the subsequent chapters that focus on strategies for achieving economic autonomy in a world marked by currency restraints.

CHAPTER 3

THE CONCEPT OF INCOME MULTIPLICITY

3.1 Defining Income Multiplicity

Income multiplicity, at its essence, refers to the strategic diversification of sources of income within an economy or for an individual. It involves cultivating a range of revenue streams that are not only varied in nature but also possess a degree of independence from one another. This intentional diversification is a proactive approach to mitigate risks associated with economic uncertainties, including those arising from currency controls.

3.1.1 Holistic Approach to Income

Income multiplicity is more than just the accumulation of income from different sectors; it is a holistic approach that takes into account the interconnectedness of economic activities. It involves diversifying income not only across sectors but also across geographical regions, industries, and asset classes. By doing so, individuals and nations can create a robust and resilient economic foundation.

3.1.2 Independence of Income Streams

A key element of income multiplicity is the independence of income streams. This means that the success or failure of one source of income does not unduly impact the viability of others. For instance, a country heavily dependent on a single export commodity may face significant challenges if the global demand or prices for that commodity fluctuate. Income multiplicity aims to break such dependencies, ensuring that economic shocks are absorbed more evenly.

3.2 Importance in the Context of Currency Controls

In the context of currency controls, income multiplicity becomes a strategic imperative. Currency controls can introduce uncertainties in international trade, limit access to foreign markets, and impact the value of a nation's currency. In such an environment, a diversified income portfolio acts as a bulwark against the adverse effects of currency controls.

3.2.1 Mitigating Exchange Rate Risks

Currency controls often result in fluctuations in exchange rates, affecting the competitiveness of exports and the cost of imports. A diversified income base can help mitigate these risks by allowing a nation to earn income in different currencies and reducing its reliance on a single export or import market.

3.2.2 Resilience to Capital Flight

Capital controls may restrict the flow of funds in and out of a country, impacting investment and economic growth. Income multiplicity provides a buffer against capital flight by ensuring that a nation's economic well-being is not overly reliant on a specific type of investment or foreign capital.

3.2.3 Balancing Trade Dependencies

Currency controls can disrupt international trade relations, especially if a nation is heavily dependent on a single trading partner. Income multiplicity encourages the diversification of trade relationships, reducing vulnerability to disruptions caused by changes in currency policies or trade restrictions.

3.3 Diversifying Income Streams for Resilience

The concept of income multiplicity extends beyond mitigating the impact of currency controls; it is a fundamental strategy for building economic resilience. This section explores how diversifying income streams contributes to resilience in the face of broader economic challenges.

3.3.1 Economic Stability in Times of Crisis

During economic crises, certain industries may be disproportionately affected. Income multiplicity ensures that the overall economic stability of a nation is not compromised by the downturn of a specific sector. For example, a nation heavily reliant on tourism may face severe economic challenges during a global pandemic, while a diversified economy with multiple income streams can better weather the storm.

3.3.2 Job Creation and Social Stability

Diversifying income streams often involves the development of various industries, leading to increased job opportunities. A diverse job market contributes to social stability by reducing dependency on specific sectors and providing individuals with alternative avenues for employment.

3.3.3 Sustainable Development

Income multiplicity aligns with the principles of sustainable development by promoting a balanced and diversified economy. By avoiding overreliance on finite resources or a single sector, nations can pursue economic growth without compromising environmental and social sustainability.

3.4 Examples of Successful Income Multiplicity

Examining real-world examples of nations that have successfully implemented income multiplicity provides valuable insights into the tangible benefits of this approach.

3.4.1 Norway: Sovereign Wealth Fund and Energy Sector

Norway's success in income multiplicity is exemplified by its Sovereign Wealth Fund, which is fueled by revenues from the country's oil and gas sector. Rather than relying solely on oil exports, Norway has strategically diversified its income by investing in a globally diversified portfolio. This approach has shielded the nation from the volatility of energy markets and created a sustainable source of income for future generations.

3.4.2 Singapore: Diverse Economic Ecosystem

Singapore's economic success is attributed to its diversified income streams across various sectors. While it started as a trading hub,

Singapore has strategically developed industries such as finance, technology, and logistics. The country's economic resilience is evident in its ability to adapt to changing global dynamics and maintain consistent growth.

3.4.3 Costa Rica: Eco-Tourism and Technology

Costa Rica has embraced income multiplicity by capitalizing on both its natural resources and technological capabilities. The country's commitment to eco-tourism and the development of its technology sector has created a balanced income portfolio. This strategy has not only contributed to economic growth but has also positioned Costa Rica as a leader in sustainable development.

These examples underscore the versatility of income multiplicity as a strategy for economic autonomy. By diversifying income streams, nations can navigate the complexities of global economic challenges, including those posed by currency controls, and build a foundation for sustained growth and resilience. In conclusion, Chapter 3 has explored the concept of income multiplicity, defining its parameters and highlighting its importance, particularly in the context of currency controls. By examining the strategic advantages of income multiplicity and showcasing real-world examples of successful implementation, this chapter sets the stage for the subsequent exploration of strategies for achieving economic autonomy in a world characterized by currency restraints.

CHAPTER 4

STRATEGIES FOR ECONOMIC AUTONOMY

In the pursuit of economic autonomy, nations must deploy a multifaceted approach that addresses legal, regulatory, financial, entrepreneurial, and diplomatic dimensions. This chapter delineates key strategies for achieving economic autonomy in the face of currency controls, emphasizing the need for a comprehensive and adaptive approach.

4.1 Legal and Regulatory Considerations

4.1.1 Currency Control Reforms

Effective legal and regulatory frameworks are indispensable for achieving economic autonomy. Nations must periodically review and reform their currency control policies to strike a balance between facilitating international trade and protecting their economic interests. This involves creating an environment that encourages foreign investment, streamlines cross-border transactions, and fosters economic growth.

Reforms may include easing restrictions on foreign currency transactions, providing clearer guidelines for international trade, and implementing measures to prevent illicit financial activities. A transparent and adaptive legal framework enhances a nation's attractiveness to foreign investors and contributes to a robust economic ecosystem.

4.1.2 Investor-Friendly Legislation

To attract foreign direct investment (FDI) and promote domestic entrepreneurship, nations should enact investor-friendly legislation. This involves creating legal structures that protect property rights, ensure fair dispute resolution mechanisms, and facilitate the ease of doing business. Legal certainty and a stable regulatory environment contribute significantly to economic autonomy by encouraging long-term investments and fostering a conducive atmosphere for business development.

Additionally, governments can explore the implementation of special economic zones with tailored regulations to attract specific industries or types of investment. These zones can serve as incubators for economic growth, innovation, and job creation.

4.2 Developing Robust Domestic Financial Systems

4.2.1 Strengthening Banking and Financial Infrastructure

A robust domestic financial system is a cornerstone of economic autonomy. Nations should focus on strengthening their banking and financial infrastructure to support sustainable economic growth. This involves fostering a stable and competitive banking sector, implementing effective monetary policies, and promoting financial inclusion.

Ensuring the stability of the banking sector includes measures to prevent financial crises, such as adequate regulatory oversight, risk management protocols, and stress testing. Furthermore, the development of a modern and efficient payment system is crucial for facilitating domestic and international transactions.

4.2.2 Sovereign Wealth Funds

Sovereign wealth funds (SWFs) can play a pivotal role in economic autonomy by serving as a reservoir of national wealth. Countries can accumulate funds from commodity exports, investments, or other revenue streams and strategically manage these assets to generate long-term returns.

Norway's Government Pension Fund Global, funded by oil revenues, serves as an exemplary model of a well-managed sovereign wealth fund that contributes to economic stability and autonomy.

The establishment and prudent management of SWFs require clear legal frameworks, governance structures, and transparency to build trust with investors and citizens alike.

4.3 Fostering Entrepreneurship and Innovation

4.3.1 Creating a Supportive Ecosystem

Economic autonomy thrives on entrepreneurship and innovation. Governments can foster a conducive environment for entrepreneurs by simplifying bureaucratic processes, offering financial incentives, and providing access to mentorship and resources. Creating incubators, accelerators, and innovation hubs can cultivate a culture of entrepreneurship and empower individuals to transform innovative ideas into viable businesses.

Investments in education and skills development are also instrumental in nurturing a workforce equipped for the demands of a rapidly evolving global economy. By fostering a culture of creativity and adaptability, nations can position themselves at the forefront of technological advancements and economic innovation.

4.3.2 Public-Private Partnerships

Collaboration between the public and private sectors is essential for promoting entrepreneurship and innovation. Governments can establish public-private partnerships (PPPs) to leverage the strengths of both sectors, sharing risks and resources. PPPs can facilitate infrastructure development, research initiatives, and technology transfer, contributing to economic diversification and autonomy.

Encouraging corporate responsibility and supporting initiatives that promote social entrepreneurship can further enhance the positive impact of the private sector on economic development.

4.4 Strengthening Trade Alliances and Bilateral Agreements

4.4.1 Diversifying Trade Partnerships

To navigate the challenges posed by currency controls, nations should actively diversify their trade partnerships. Overdependence on a single trading partner can make a nation vulnerable to economic disruptions. By diversifying trade relationships, countries reduce their exposure to external shocks and enhance their ability to adapt to changing economic conditions.

Participating in regional and global trade agreements, such as free trade agreements (FTAs) and customs unions, can open new avenues for economic growth and facilitate the movement of goods and services across borders. These agreements often include provisions to mitigate currency-related risks and enhance economic cooperation.

4.4.2 Bilateral Agreements and Economic Diplomacy

Bilateral agreements play a crucial role in enhancing economic autonomy. Nations can engage in strategic negotiations with key partners to foster mutually beneficial economic relationships. These agreements may include provisions for currency swaps, trade facilitation measures, and cooperation on economic development projects.

Moreover, effective economic diplomacy can strengthen a nation's position in the global economic landscape. By building diplomatic ties and engaging in dialogue with other nations, countries can promote their economic interests, attract foreign investment, and establish collaborative frameworks for addressing shared challenges.

In conclusion, Chapter 4 outlines a comprehensive set of strategies for achieving economic autonomy in the context of currency controls. By addressing legal and regulatory considerations, developing robust domestic financial systems, fostering entrepreneurship and innovation, and strengthening trade alliances and bilateral agreements, nations can position themselves to navigate the challenges of a dynamic global economy while building resilience and sustainability.

The successful implementation of these strategies requires a coordinated and adaptive approach, reflecting the interconnected nature of economic autonomy in the contemporary world.

CHAPTER 5
CASE STUDIES: NATIONS ACHIEVING ECONOMIC AUTONOMY

Case studies offer valuable insights into the practical implementation of strategies for economic autonomy. This chapter examines the experiences of Singapore, Norway, and Costa Rica—nations that have successfully navigated economic challenges, including those related to currency controls. By delving into their unique approaches, this chapter aims to distill lessons that can be applied by other nations seeking to enhance their economic autonomy.

5.1 Singapore: A Model of Economic Autonomy

5.1.1 Diversification Across Industries

Singapore's economic success is emblematic of a nation that has strategically diversified its income streams and embraced economic autonomy. Historically reliant on trade, Singapore has expanded its economic portfolio to include finance, technology, manufacturing, and logistics.

This diversification has enabled the country to weather global economic downturns and position itself as a resilient and adaptable economy.

The government's pro-business policies, low tax rates, and efficient regulatory environment have attracted multinational corporations and fostered a vibrant ecosystem for entrepreneurship and innovation. Singapore's commitment to maintaining a competitive edge in various industries exemplifies the importance of flexibility and adaptability in achieving economic autonomy.

5.1.2 Strategic Investment in Human Capital

Singapore places a strong emphasis on education and skills development as a cornerstone of economic autonomy. The nation has consistently invested in developing a highly skilled and adaptable workforce, aligning educational programs with the needs of emerging industries. This strategic approach to human capital development ensures that Singapore remains at the forefront of technological advancements and can readily adapt to changing global economic landscapes.

5.1.3 Economic Diplomacy and Trade Alliances

Singapore's success in economic diplomacy and its active participation in trade alliances have contributed significantly to its economic autonomy.

The nation has forged strong trade relationships with a diverse range of partners, reducing its dependence on any single market. Additionally, Singapore's commitment to free trade agreements and open markets has facilitated the movement of goods and services, further enhancing its economic resilience.

5.2 Norway: Balancing Natural Resources and Diversification

5.2.1 Sovereign Wealth Fund Management

Norway's economic autonomy is exemplified by its management of the Government Pension Fund Global, one of the world's largest sovereign wealth funds. Fueled by revenues from the oil and gas sector, Norway has demonstrated a commitment to responsible and sustainable fund management. The fund serves as a financial buffer against volatile oil prices and provides a stable source of income for the nation.

The establishment of clear legal frameworks, transparent governance structures, and ethical investment principles has been instrumental in building trust in Norway's sovereign wealth fund. This case underscores the importance of sound financial management in achieving economic autonomy.

5.2.2 Diversification Beyond Natural Resources

While Norway has harnessed the economic benefits of its natural resources, it has also recognized the importance of diversification. The country has invested in renewable energy, technology, and other sectors to reduce its reliance on oil and gas. This strategic diversification contributes to long-term economic sustainability and resilience in the face of changing global energy dynamics.

5.2.3 Social and Economic Inclusion

Norway's focus on social and economic inclusion has played a pivotal role in achieving economic autonomy. The nation's commitment to a comprehensive social welfare system, high-quality education, and inclusive economic policies has created a society with high levels of human capital and social cohesion. This holistic approach to development reinforces the resilience of Norway's economy and contributes to its long-term stability.

5.3 Costa Rica: Embracing Sustainable Development

5.3.1 Eco-Tourism and Biodiversity

Costa Rica stands out as a nation that has embraced sustainable development as a key pillar of economic autonomy. The country's commitment to eco-tourism, coupled with the preservation of its rich biodiversity, has positioned Costa Rica as a leader in environmentally conscious economic practices. By capitalizing on its natural assets, Costa Rica has not only attracted international visitors but has also fostered sustainable economic growth.

5.3.2 Technology and Innovation

Costa Rica's strategic focus on technology and innovation has contributed to economic diversification. The country has positioned itself as a hub for technology and business process outsourcing, attracting global companies seeking a favorable business environment. The government's support for research and development initiatives and the cultivation of a skilled workforce underscore the importance of forward-looking policies in achieving economic autonomy.

5.3.3 Commitment to Education and Healthcare

Costa Rica's investment in education and healthcare has played a crucial role in building human capital and promoting social well-being. By ensuring access to quality education and healthcare services, the nation has created a workforce that is competitive in the global marketplace. This commitment to human development aligns with the principles of sustainable and inclusive economic growth.

5.4 Lessons Learned and Applicability to Other Nations

5.4.1 Flexibility and Adaptability

The case studies of Singapore, Norway, and Costa Rica highlight the importance of flexibility and adaptability in achieving economic autonomy. These nations have demonstrated the ability to pivot and diversify their economic activities in response to changing global dynamics. Flexibility in policies, openness to innovation, and a willingness to embrace new industries are critical factors that other nations can draw upon in their pursuit of economic autonomy.

5.4.2 Strategic Management of Natural Resources

For countries endowed with natural resources, the strategic management of these assets is paramount. Norway's approach to managing its sovereign wealth fund, in particular, serves as a model for responsible resource utilization. Clear legal frameworks, transparent governance, and ethical investment principles can guide other nations in ensuring that natural resources contribute to long-term economic stability.

5.4.3 Holistic Development Strategies

The case studies underscore the importance of holistic development strategies that go beyond economic considerations. Investments in education, healthcare, and social inclusion are integral components of building resilient societies and workforces. By prioritizing human development alongside economic growth, nations can create the foundation for sustained economic autonomy.

5.4.4 Diplomacy and Trade Relationships

Economic diplomacy and the cultivation of diverse trade relationships are critical elements of achieving economic autonomy. Singapore's active participation in trade alliances, Norway's strategic economic diplomacy, and Costa Rica's efforts to attract international businesses showcase the diplomatic dimensions of economic success.

By fostering positive diplomatic ties and diversifying trade partnerships, nations can enhance their economic resilience.

In conclusion, the case studies presented in this chapter offer valuable lessons for nations seeking to enhance their economic autonomy. The experiences of Singapore, Norway, and Costa Rica demonstrate the effectiveness of diverse strategies, including diversification across industries, strategic management of natural resources, and a holistic approach to development. By drawing on these lessons, nations can craft tailored approaches that align with their unique contexts and challenges, ultimately contributing to greater economic autonomy in an ever-evolving global landscape.

CHAPTER 6

OVERCOMING CHALLENGES AND BUILDING A RESILIENT FUTURE

In the pursuit of economic autonomy, nations encounter a myriad of challenges, ranging from currency controls and trade imbalances to global economic uncertainties. This chapter delves into the identification of common challenges, explores strategies for building resilience, emphasizes the role of international collaboration, and provides recommendations for governments and businesses seeking to navigate the complex landscape of economic autonomy.

6.1 Identifying Common Challenges

6.1.1 Currency Controls and Trade Barriers

One of the primary challenges nations face in achieving economic autonomy is the imposition of currency controls and trade barriers. These measures can disrupt international trade, limit access to foreign markets, and introduce uncertainties in the global economic landscape. For nations heavily reliant on exports or with significant foreign debt, navigating currency controls becomes particularly challenging.

6.1.2 Global Economic Uncertainties

The interconnected nature of the global economy exposes nations to uncertainties arising from economic downturns, financial crises, and geopolitical tensions. Economic uncertainties can result in fluctuations in exchange rates, volatility in commodity prices, and disruptions in international trade. These uncertainties pose challenges for economic planning and require adaptive strategies to mitigate their impact.

6.1.3 Technological Disruptions and Automation

Rapid technological advancements, including automation and artificial intelligence, present both opportunities and challenges. While automation can enhance productivity and efficiency, it may also lead to job displacement and economic inequalities.

Nations aiming for economic autonomy must navigate the complexities of technological disruptions and proactively address the societal impacts of automation.

6.1.4 Environmental Sustainability and Climate Change

Environmental sustainability has become a pressing concern for nations worldwide. The challenges posed by climate change, resource depletion, and environmental degradation require nations to balance economic development with ecological responsibility. Achieving economic autonomy necessitates strategies that promote sustainable practices and mitigate the environmental impact of economic activities.

6.2 Resilience in the Face of Global Economic Uncertainties

6.2.1 Diversification of Income Sources

Building economic resilience involves a strategic focus on diversifying income sources. Nations can mitigate the impact of currency controls and trade uncertainties by cultivating a portfolio of industries that are not overly dependent on a single market or commodity. Diversification provides a buffer against economic shocks, ensuring that the nation's income is derived from a variety of sources.

6.2.2 Adaptive Economic Policies

Resilience requires governments to adopt adaptive economic policies that can respond to changing global conditions. Flexibility in monetary and fiscal policies, along with a willingness to embrace innovation, enables nations to navigate economic uncertainties effectively. Policymakers must be proactive in identifying emerging challenges and formulating strategies that position the nation for resilience and growth.

6.2.3 Investment in Human Capital

The resilience of a nation is closely tied to the skills and adaptability of its workforce. Investments in education, vocational training, and lifelong learning programs contribute to the development of a skilled and agile workforce. A highly educated and adaptable workforce can drive innovation, enhance productivity, and contribute to the nation's ability to weather economic uncertainties.

6.2.4 Social Safety Nets

Robust social safety nets play a crucial role in building resilience, particularly during economic downturns. Governments can establish comprehensive social welfare programs that provide support to vulnerable populations, ensuring that citizens have access to healthcare, education, and basic necessities. Social safety nets contribute to social stability and reduce the impact of economic shocks on the most vulnerable segments of society.

6.3 The Role of International Collaboration

6.3.1 Multilateralism in Trade Relations

In a globalized world, international collaboration is integral to economic autonomy. Nations can pursue multilateral agreements and participate in international organizations to strengthen trade relations and address common challenges. By fostering an environment of cooperation, nations can navigate the complexities of currency controls and trade barriers, creating a more predictable and stable global economic landscape.

6.3.2 Knowledge Sharing and Innovation Networks

International collaboration extends to knowledge sharing and innovation networks. Nations can benefit from collaborative research initiatives, technology transfer agreements, and partnerships that foster innovation and technological advancements. By participating in global innovation networks, nations can leverage collective expertise to address challenges and propel economic development.

6.3.3 Climate Change Mitigation and Sustainable Development Goals

Environmental challenges require a collaborative approach. Nations can engage in international efforts to mitigate climate change, uphold sustainable development goals, and share best practices in environmental conservation. Collaborative initiatives can lead to the development of innovative solutions, technological advancements, and policy frameworks that contribute to global sustainability and economic autonomy.

6.4 Recommendations for Governments and Businesses

6.4.1 Agile Policy Formulation and Implementation

Governments must prioritize agile policy formulation and implementation to adapt to the dynamic nature of the global economy. This involves regular assessments of economic conditions, proactive identification of challenges, and the swift implementation of policies that support resilience and sustainable growth. A responsive and forward-looking government is key to navigating the complexities of economic autonomy.

6.4.2 Investment in Education and Innovation

Governments should prioritize investments in education and innovation to build a skilled and creative workforce. By fostering a culture of continuous learning and innovation, nations can position themselves at the forefront of technological advancements and enhance their economic competitiveness. Businesses, in turn, should actively participate in collaborative research and development initiatives to drive innovation.

6.4.3 Corporate Social Responsibility (CSR) and Sustainability

Businesses play a crucial role in promoting economic autonomy through responsible corporate practices. Adopting corporate social responsibility (CSR) initiatives that prioritize environmental sustainability, ethical business practices, and community engagement contributes to the overall resilience of the business environment. Sustainability-focused businesses are better positioned to navigate changing consumer preferences and global environmental concerns.

6.4.4 International Engagement and Diplomacy

Both governments and businesses should actively engage in international diplomacy to foster positive relationships and collaborations. Building strong diplomatic ties contributes to economic resilience by facilitating trade agreements, addressing global challenges, and creating a conducive environment for international investments. Proactive international engagement enhances a nation's and businesses' ability to navigate the complexities of a globalized economy.

In conclusion, Chapter 6 outlines the challenges faced by nations in their pursuit of economic autonomy and provides strategies for building resilience in the face of uncertainties. By identifying common challenges, promoting resilience through diversified income sources and adaptive policies, emphasizing the role of international collaboration, and offering recommendations for governments and businesses, this chapter aims to guide nations on a path towards a more resilient and economically autonomous future.

In an ever-changing global landscape, the ability to overcome challenges and build a resilient future is paramount for sustained economic growth and development.